EMPOWERED
For The Wait

EMPOWERED
For The Wait

Don't Settle as You Wait for Your Mate

Charmia Martin

Charmia MARTIN
MINISTRIES

Charmia Martin © 2021

ISBN: 978-1-7371210-0-8

Because of the dynamic nature of the internet, any web addresses or links contained in this book may have changed since publication and may no longer be valid. The views expressed in this work are solely those of the author and do not necessarily reflect the views of the publisher, and the publisher disclaims any responsibility for them.

Printed in the United States of America   0 7 3 0 2 1

♾ This paper meets the requirements of ANSI/NISO Z39.48-1992 (Permanence of Paper)

Visit www.charmiamartin.com/resources
*for free resources to help you be
Empowered for the Wait*

CONTENTS

INTRODUCTION

Thank you for purchasing my book and allowing me to join you on this journey. During the wait, it's so easy to become frustrated or tired, or you just might begin to feel that you want to marry the next person who shows a slight bit of interest in you. You may think, like, *hello, go ahead and ask me already!*

If you are not careful, you'll fall into that dreadful trap of comparing yourself with others and falling for the myth that God loves others more than He loves you. Then, pretty soon, rejection and fear will try to rob you of your confidence in God and make you think that you have to compromise on your standards to secure a mate.

I can relate. I, too, believed the lie. I was caught up thinking that I had to take my life into my own hands. I began to think, *If I don't help God, it's not going to happen.* Then, I learned the truth that God loves me. I learned that He loves all of me, and I was not alone. I discovered that His love for me dismantles all fear, and His acceptance of me uproots all seeds of rejection. He showed me that my body can be a dwelling place for the Holy Spirit, and my marriage will be for His glory.

After the first five years of praying for a mate and remaining single, I finally realized that I couldn't be a helpmeet until I helped "me". It was time for me to take advantage of my waiting season and stop allowing my waiting season to take advantage of me.

I knew how to be single, but I was still broken.

I knew how to be broken but was afraid of being whole.

I knew how to act like I was satisfied but not content.

I knew how to act like I was happy, but inside, I struggled with being happy for others.

I knew how to repeat cycles while desiring a true change on the inside.

Therefore, I turned to the Author and Finisher of my faith. When I encountered the One, I stopped searching for the one. Then, I became one with Him, which gave me grace to become the person I desired to attract. This experience revolutionized my life. I learned that God is near to all those who call upon His name. That's why I wrote this book. I wrote this book to remind you that God is faithful, and He will give you the desires of your heart at the appointed time. Get ready to be empowered, inspired, and propelled into your NOW season of faith, so you will never settle.

Grab your tissue, pen, and journal and let's go on a journey from being anxious and frustrated to excited and postured in expectation for your mate.

CHAPTER 1

Tired of The Wait

*"For I know the thoughts that I think toward you,
says the Lord, thoughts of peace and not of evil,
to give you an expected end."*
– Jeremiah 29:11 KJV

Have you ever asked yourself this question, *why not me?* Then, you answer the question with a limited view of what's going on around you instead of focusing on what God is doing in you. For example, you may say, *all my friends are married, and I am still single. Then, you rationalize with yourself by saying, "I'm a good person. I volunteer three times a week. I have a great life. I have a decent career. My morning devotional is everything. I attend church two times a week. I do everything right. I know that I am pleasing God; even my speech pleases God. I encourage others even when I don't feel encouraged. I search for ways to make others feel good even when I don't feel good.* I was rehearsing all these things in my mind trying to prove to myself that I have earned my request because of my behavior. You know the type of behavior that allows us to hide how we really feel and moves us away from being our true selves.

It's easy to become tired in the wait when we believe our waiting is contingent upon our actions. In other words, we believe the better I behave, the more I can expect from God. We also could feel that the worse I behave, the less I can expect from God. While we do reap what we sow in this world (see Galatians 6:9), we must examine our motives. You see, it's not necessarily the "what" but the "why" behind our request that must be revealed. We must ask ourselves, *could I be tired of waiting because I feel that the things, I have accomplished in life make me worthy of having whatever I ask from God? Am I tired because I'm waiting on others, or am I really tired of waiting on God? Could it be that I desire life on my terms instead of God's plan?*

We must examine our motives as well as our posture. Let's deal with our motives first. The Bible tells us in the book of James chapter 4:3 "ye ask, and receive not, because ye ask amiss, that ye consume it upon your lusts." *Let me ask you again, why are you tired of the wait? Is it because you are tired of being the only one of your friends who is still single? Are you tired of being lonely on Valentine's Day? Are you tired of being the only one paying your bills? Is it because your biological clock is ticking? Is it because you want to talk to someone consistently? Could it be because your child or children need a parental figure? Maybe, you would like to have someone sit next to you at church? Moreover, the most famous reason for them all is that it would be great to have someone with whom you can have SEX from time to time.*

While these questions are not the complete list of motives that we may have, you must ask the Holy Spirit to reveal and purify your motives.

I've learned from experience that impure motives were the root cause of my tiredness and fueled much of my frustration during my waiting season. I remember asking the Lord daily for a mate. I also remember going to the altar asking the pastor to agree with me that God would send my mate. The pastor smiled and said, "God is not finished preparing you for your mate." I walked away sad and discouraged trying to figure out why God was not finished preparing me for my mate. I am a saved woman who loves Jesus, lives righteously, and allows the Holy Spirit to orchestrate my life. Two years later, I asked my prayer partner, "Why do you believe that I am not married?" She smiled and said, "You are still single because if God was to send you a husband now, you would make him your god and forget about raising your daughter." I was offended by her comment and immediately asked her if I could call her back. After that conversation, I fell to my knees asking the Lord to reveal my heart. Then, out of my soul, I began to write down all these reasons why I wanted a mate.

- I wanted someone to love me.
- I wanted someone to love my daughter.
- I wanted someone to assist with paying my bills.
- I wanted someone to attend church and social gatherings with me.
- I wanted someone to make me feel special.
- I wanted someone to hold me when I was afraid.

I just wanted someone to want me. That was it. That was the root. If I didn't have a man in my life, I felt unwanted.

Right now, I would like to challenge each of you to take a moment and ask the Holy Spirit to reveal your heart to you. Why are you really tired? Why do you really desire a mate? Then, be honest with yourself and identify the root.

For me, I just wanted to be loved. The truth is no one can love us like Jesus. No one can make us feel accepted like the Lord. In actuality, I was searching for someone to be my god instead of looking for a person who would remind me of the goodness of God. I was searching for someone to validate me when I was already validated by God. I was searching for someone to love me when all I had to do was receive God's love without trying to earn His love and approval. I was searching for someone to pay my bills when God said that He would take care of my needs. I was searching for someone with whom I could attend functions only to realize that the Lord is always with me. I was searching for someone to make me feel special when the Lord said I am chosen to bring Him glory. I was searching for someone to protect me when the Lord is my shield and protector, and I have no reason to fear because He is with me.

For those next couple of months, I searched for scriptures in the Bible that reminded me of God's love towards me. I meditated on those scriptures until I was able to close the curtains to what was missing in my life and began enjoying what was already in my life. For me, my singleness was a time in my life during which the Lord was my

Knight in shining armor who protected me in my waiting season. He protected me from myself. He protected me from marrying someone for the wrong reasons, and with the help of the Holy Spirit, I was able to purify my reasons for desiring to be married.

- I should get married because my husband and I can do more together than apart.
- I should get married because I desire to help my mate fulfill his Kingdom mandate.
- I should get married because I have exhausted my single-hood.
- I should get married because I understand my weaknesses and recognize how we can complement each other.

Even while I was writing this book, God was purifying my motives. Am I writing this book so I can look good or am I writing this book so God can be glorified? In everything, we should desire to bring glory to God.

When our motives change, our posture changes. We stop viewing ourselves as a defeated person but as a child of the Most High God. Our posture has a lot to do with our soul and the manner in which we process things through the lenses of our life. There-fore, we must upgrade our soul to believe that the Lord doesn't mind us being married, and we must believe that He has our best interest at heart. It's not that God is not answering our prayers. If our motives are pure and we have scripture about what we are praying, we have confidence in knowing that our prayers will be answered. Even though what you have asked for is being delayed, you must still believe that you will not be denied. Having decided to believe, you'll begin to feel strengthened in your inner man, which will fuel your expectancy instead of your fatigue.

I challenge you today to search the scriptures and begin to repeat and say what God says about you. Only you know the true root of your tiredness, and once it is revealed, begin applying the Word of God to your situation. Below are some scriptures to get you started.

SCRIPTURES:

"For God so loved the world, that He gave his only begotten Son, that whosoever believeth in Him should not perish, but have everlasting life."
–John 3:16 KJV

"To the praise of the glory of His grace, wherein He hath made us accepted in the beloved."
–Ephesian 1:6 KJV

"But ye are a chosen generation, a royal priesthood, a holy nation, a peculiar people; that ye should shew forth the praises of Him who hath called you out of darkness into His marvelous light."
–1 Peter 2:9 KJV

Prayer

Lord, help me not to become weary in well doing because You said that at the appointed time, which was predestined before the foundation of this world, I will reap if I faint not. Thank you, Father, for supplying me with Your strength and endurance to continue serving and living for You while I wait for the fulfillment of Your promise. In Jesus's name. Amen.

CHAPTER 2

You Are Not Alone

"Whither shall I go from thy spirit? Or whither shall I flee from thy presence? If I ascend up into heaven, thou art there; if I make my bed in hell, behold, thou art there."
–Psalm 139:7-8 KJV

I t's so easy to feel alone when we are searching for answers within ourselves instead of looking to the One, who created us, for the solution. While we may feel alone, the Bible reminds us in Hebrews 13:5 that God will "never leave us nor forsake us."

In the previous chapter, I introduced the concept of closing the curtains. When we close the curtains, we understand that we are not alone, and we are becoming one with the Father. This means that we're not focusing on what's going on around us, but we are taking inventory of what's happening inside us. In these times when you are feeling lonely, and loneliness tries to consume you, challenge yourself to run towards God instead of running away from Him.

Some of us have to fight the temptation of giving our bodies permission to search for love in all the wrong places. We also must fight the temptation of pursuing earthly recognition by earning degrees, promotions, and titles, so we can be celebrated by man but no longer be recognized by God. Oftentimes, we volunteer to help everyone, and we are present at every event doing everything we can to avoid being by ourselves. We call it occupying or doing business until the Lord's return (see Luke 19:13), but in actuality, we're trying to keep busy to avoid embracing our true self.

You must begin asking yourself the right questions to address the true root cause of your loneliness. Ask yourself, *am I feeling lonely because I feel inadequate within myself? Am I lonely when my constant need for acceptance and validation is missing? Could it be that I have not accepted whose I am and who God created me to be?* Those were just some sample questions, but you must dig deeper and ask the Holy Spirit to reveal the root cause to you. I know you're saying that you are fine, but are you really fine? When was the last time you were able to turn off the television and have some serious alone time with the Father? When was the last time you sat still and blotted out all distractions? When was the last time you said no to an event, program, or over-time at work just to spend some alone time with the Father? I'm not here to judge the length of that time or to suggest the hour of that time. However, I would like to challenge you to allow yourself to become vulnerable before your Heavenly Father. Pour out your heart before Him and reveal to Him how you really feel. Hopefully, by doing this, you will begin to discover what is causing you to feel alone. If you still find yourself struggling, it's okay to share how you feel with a trusted friend, mentor, coach, parents, or a professional counselor. In doing this, you will bring accountability and light to what the enemy has tried to keep hidden in your life. I never wanted to be by myself. I felt as though I couldn't live on my own. I couldn't dine at a restaurant on my own. To be honest, I got pregnant at eighteen because I never wanted to be alone. I said if I had a child, I would have someone who would never leave me and would always love me.

I was dealing with abandonment issues because my mother was taken from me when I was ten years old. She was 27 years old and found herself in an abusive relationship. When she tried to escape that relationship, she ended up in a body bag. My mother's life was taken too soon, and she left behind two daughters who were trying to make sense of the world. Therefore, as I grew up, I was searching for a mother in everyone I met. This search for acceptance caused me to open myself up to manipulation, and I allowed others to control me instead of being led by the Holy Spirit. Even after the birth of my daughter, I still longed for more acceptance and validation, and I wrestled with those feelings of loneliness.

Additionally, I quickly learned that having a baby required more responsibility and wholeness from me to form a healthy attachment with my child. Therefore, I found myself struggling to raise my daughter because I couldn't give her what I didn't have. I found myself struggling in relationships because I was suffocating all my friendships and those who came into my life.

As I struggled to raise my daughter and find someone to love me, so I wouldn't feel alone, I finally decided that I no longer could live like this. I fell on my knees and asked Jesus to heal my heart. After asking Jesus to heal my heart, I began to repent for searching for love in all the wrong places. Then, I received my sonship. In order to embrace your true sonship, you must take the time to allow the Holy Spirit to reveal whose you are and who

God created you to be. We don't have to live like an orphan and allow loneliness and rejection to be our portion because we have a Heavenly Father who says that "He will never leave us nor forsake us" (see Hebrews 13:5).

I challenge you to begin to search the scriptures and ask the Holy Spirit to reveal your true identity to you. Allow the Holy Spirit to reveal to you the love of the Father and take time to receive His love, acceptance, and validation. Below are some scriptures to get you started.

SCRIPTURES:

"Having predestinated us unto the adoption of children by Jesus Christ to himself, according to the good pleasure of His will,"
–Ephesians 1:5 KJV

"To the praise of the glory of His grace, wherein He hath made us accepted in the beloved."
–Ephesians 1:6 KJV

"For He hath said, I will never leave thee, nor forsake thee."
–Hebrews 13:5 KJV

Prayer

Lord, open the eyes of my heart that I may exalt You above anything and everything that comes my way. Father, consume and overtake me with Your love, so the spirit of loneliness will be broken off my life and off the life of my children's children. Thank you, Father, that Your joy always will be my banner against loneliness, feelings of inadequacy, and self-doubt. I receive Your adoption, and I take my place as a son or daughter of the Most High God. In Jesus's name. Amen.

CHAPTER 3

Breaking the Cycle of Comparison

*"For I am fearfully and wonderfully made: marvelous are
thy works; and that my soul knoweth right well."*
–Psalm 139:14 KJV

I t is so easy for us to get stuck in the comparison trap. That's when we begin comparing ourselves with others instead of examining ourselves against the Word of God. We tend to say these things to explain why we are not married. *If my skin was a little lighter, I would have been married by now. If I had a smaller or a larger waistline, I would have been married by now. If I would have joined that church with all the men, I would have been married by now. If my nose, legs, bottom, or upper extremities were smaller or larger, I would have been married by now. If I would've had both parents in my household, I would have been married by now. If my parents hadn't divorced, I would have been married by now. If I wasn't a single parent, I would have been married by now. If I would have gone to an Ivy League college, I would have been married by* now. If I had gone to all the right places where everyone else goes or the best hangouts, I would have been married by now. If I had been popular in college, I would have been married by now.

The truth of the matter is that all the "ifs" and "would haves" can cause us to devalue what God finds valuable about us. "You are fearfully and wonderfully made" (see Psalm 139:14). "You are the apple of God's eye" (see Psalm 17:8). You are so valuable to God that He gave His only begotten Son for you (see John 3:16).

Say this with me. *I am valuable to God. He has made me His original. There's no need for comparison. I am not arrogant. I am confident in the Creator who created all things and fashioned me after Himself.*

Get this! God didn't wait for us to change or adjust our outward appearance before extending His love towards us. His desire is for us to experience true acceptance, which is founded upon the revelation of the Father's love.

Therefore, when our eyes are opened to the true essence of who God is and who He created us to be, it will suffocate our need to compare ourselves to others and will break the cycle of comparison. It's okay for us to make peace with our weaknesses. It's okay for us to desire change in areas of our life we can change. It's okay for us to release the prayer of serenity to make peace with those areas we cannot change. Yet, by allowing God through the power of the Holy Spirit, change can come to those areas we deemed impossible. While we can't change our past, we can change our future.

That means that you are not losing weight and building muscle, so you can attract a mate. That means that you are not trying to look or act like someone else or change yourself just for the purpose of attracting a mate. Besides, you don't want to attract just anyone. You want to attract royalty, so he or she can speak to the queen or king in you. Therefore, in everything that you do, do it for the glory of God because you are led by the Spirit of God. Hallelujah! Glory to God!

Don't get me wrong. There's nothing wrong with enhancing your outer appearance, but never forget that it's the inner you where God dwells that brings you value. It's the inner you that makes a difference. It's the inner you that's going to sustain your relationship. It's the inner you that people may not see on the outside, but it has a way of illuminating from your inside to your outside. As a result of God shining inside you, when people see you, they have a chance to see our Heavenly Father expressed through you. Your very presence will remind them of His goodness. Not only do you remind them of God's goodness, but also you remind them of His faithfulness because He keeps His word. "He will beautify the meek with salvation" (see Psalm 149:4). You have liberty in Christ but not to behave disorderly. You are free to be who He created you to be without comparison.

Say it out loud. *I am royalty. I am a King's kid. I am chosen. I am valuable! I am sufficient in Christ's sufficiency.*

MY STORY:

I remember when my husband and I submitted to the courtship process. This meant that we had already taken the time to pray about each other before we went on any dates. No, I wasn't going on any dates until I knew that he was compatible with my soul. Now, don't get me wrong. We both remained prayerful and were willing to end the relationship if we felt as though we were causing each other to stumble. We'll discuss more about our stumbles in a later chapter. There was a certain young lady who requested prayer after each service, and she only asked my soon-to-be future husband to pray for her. Immediately, I felt threatened. I started comparing my figure against her figure. I compared my hair extensions against her long silky dark hair, and before I knew it, I had fallen for the comparison trap and was devaluing what God had deemed valuable, ME! Not only that, but I was also becoming upset with the devil and blaming him for putting that woman in my future husband's path. Then, I cried out to the Lord asking Him, *why would You set me up to fail? Why would You present this fine, handsome, chocolate man to me only to have another woman walk away with him.* Get this. I am very competitive by nature, so I like a good challenge, but in this case, I couldn't get past the comparison trap. Therefore, I had to declare a fast, and after much praying and fasting, I received a revelation. It was this. There always will be someone who will be smaller or larger than me. There always will be someone with longer or shorter hair than me. However, no one, I mean no one could beat me at being me. God had made me an original. Can't nobody beat Charmia at being Charmia.

Say that with me. *Nobody can beat (say your name) at being (say your name)! You are an original.*

After that, I was no longer bothered by other women pursuing my future husband. I knew no one could cause me to devalue myself unless I agreed to allow that to happen. Therefore, we must fall out of agreement with any negative perceptions of ourselves and do the work to change anything that is in our physical realm of control.

I challenge you today to begin to create your own affirmations. You may use some affirmations from this book, but I know the Holy Spirit has some specific ones He would like for you to decree and declare over your life. You are victorious. I hear the Lord saying that you are in transition. He is transitioning many of you in your thought processes in how you see yourself and how you see Him is changing. It's time for you to L.E.A.P.

- **L** - lean into your transformation experience. Embrace it.
- **E** - erase the old thinking patterns by replacing those negative thoughts with the Word of God.
- **A** - apply the Word of God to every area of your life.
- **P** - produce what God has placed inside you.

Below are some scriptures to get you started, and you can build from there. Allow the Holy Spirit to reveal to you what is needed in this hour. Remember, you are not alone. Others will experience or have experienced the same things you may be experiencing. Don't avoid the process. You are well able to overcome anything that tries to overcome you.

SCRIPTURES:

"For thou hast possessed my reins: thou hast covered me in my mother's womb. I praise You because I am fearfully and wonderfully made; Your works are wonderful; I know that full well."
–Psalm 139:13-14 KJV

"For we are His workmanship, created in Christ Jesus unto good works, which God hath before ordained that we should walk in them."
–Ephesians 2:10 KJV

Prayer

Father, thank you that You have delivered me from the comparison trap, and I no longer devalue what You deem valuable. Help me to cherish what You cherish and celebrate what You celebrate. Help me to change those things I can change and become content with things I cannot change. I look to You, my Maker and Creator! Only in You do I find the peace, rest, safety, and strength to love and accept who You created me to be. In Jesus's name! Amen

CHAPTER 4

Dismantling Fear & Rejection

"There is no fear in love; but perfect love casts out fear: because fear hath torment. He that feareth is not made perfect in love."
–1 John 4:18 KJV

Here's my personal definition of fear. Fear is like a mental distress signal sent to distract us from moving from one place to another. It comes to intimidate and paralyze us in certain areas of our lives. I'm not saying that we won't wrestle with fear from time to time, but I am saying that through the power of God, we can break the spirit of fear off our lives. Let's be honest. Who likes to live in fear of today or tomorrow? No one. Fear torments us. When we receive God's perfect love, it will bring us peace and mental tranquility. We'll discuss more about God's love in a moment. Let's talk about rejection. To me, rejection feels like access denied. Meaning that if it's something you should have, but it's blocked or intercepted, you feel rejected. Also, if we are not careful, we can interpret delay or the waiting season as rejection, but it's just preparation for what the Lord has in store for us.

Growing up without my mother left me feeling both abandoned and rejected. I found myself being a people pleaser in hopes of being accepted and loved by others. After years of doing this, I learned the hard lesson that you never can please others no matter how hard you try. God created us to be a blessing not to become the Blessor! That's His job. In pleasing God, He causes everything else to come into alignment with His will. Not to mention, in trying to please others, we diminish our visibility, so when it's time to "show up," we have misplaced the blueprint that created our uniqueness. When our attention is centered on pleasing others more than God, we place others in spaces they were never created to occupy. Then, when they fail or disappoint us because of our unrealistic expectations, we not only separate from them, but also, we separate from God because we made them a type of little "g" or idol in our lives.

If we are not careful, we can make ourselves idols because we are always thinking about ourselves. For example, if an individual shares his or her feelings or thoughts with us, somehow, the conversation ends up about us rather than the other person.

I, too, used to wrestle with this. I had to learn this, and I am still learning to remove myself off the throne and allow the Holy Spirit to rest, rule, and abide in my life.

As far as it relates to the spirit of rejection, it will have us thinking more about what others have done to us instead of what God has and is doing for us. Rejection comes to make us feel disqualified. How can we be disqualified when we are qualified and justified by the blood of Jesus? Therefore, we must uproot the spirit of rejection from our lives because of past hurts and fears and receive right now the love of the Father. In receiving the love of the Father, you decide by faith that His love is more than enough.

Say this with me. *God's love for me is unconditional, unchanging, unwavering, and always predictable because there's nothing that I can do to earn His love. God chooses to love me despite of me."*

MY STORY:

During the first ten years of my singleness, I found it was so hard to be told *not right now or you are not the one.* I remember that I went on date after date which led only to disappointment and heartbreak. It was hard for me to understand why that single man didn't pursue me. As a result, I found myself changing careers and churches as each of my relationships failed. Then, one day during prayer, I heard the Holy Spirit say, "Love thou me?" I said, "Lord, I love you." Then, I heard the Spirit say, "Do you trust me?" I said, "Lord, I trust you." The Spirit said, "Then if you trust me, why are you blaming others for closed doors when I have the ability to open them?" Instantly, the light bulb came on. Our life is in God's hands. If we love Him and He loves us, we can trust that He has our best interest at heart. God can be trusted with the pain of our past because He desires to give us pleasure in our future. Therefore, the more we evolve into who God created us to be, the more we can say man's rejection was God's redirection. God is rerouting you towards something better. Soon, you will get to the place where you learn to be comfortable with closed doors because you now understand that no man can close a door that God has opened for you. As God heals your heart from the root of rejection, your response to closed doors or what appears to be some type of rejection will be, *my God has a plan*. He is saving the best for last. Glory to God!

As I matured in God, I found myself closing some doors. I was no longer desperate for any man, and I was willing to wait for the man God destined for me. The more I learned about myself, the more I began to love myself. Then, patience kicked in, and I was willing to wait on God while remaining in Him. In your waiting season, you must continue to guard your heart with all diligence because out of it flows how you will perceive and receive life (see Proverb 4:23). Truly, we live from our heart. When our heart is healthy, we will be healthy.

We must remember that receiving God's love dismantles all fear, and the acceptance of His love destroys the root of rejection. It's not enough for us to talk about His love. We must receive it. You see, every new season or level in God requires another revelation of God's love towards you concerning what you are believing He will do for you. For me, the affirmations I stated were my thing. Every morning, in the afternoon, every night, and in front of my child I said repeatedly, *God loves me. God loves me. God loves me. Every day, I quoted Ephesians 1:6 and said," I am accepted in the beloved", which means that God accepts me, loves me, and I am His child.*

No matter what, we must tell ourselves that we are accepted. We are approved by God. The principle is this. Receiving God's love provides us with the ability to demonstrate and express His love to-wards others. In Matthew 22:39 it says that "we should love our neighbor as we love ourselves", but if we don't love ourselves, how can we love our neighbor or our future mate? How can we give others what we don't have ourselves?

ANOTHER STORY:

When my future husband and I were in courtship, I needed another revelation of God's love for me to receive Him. Therefore, I gave the Holy Spirit per-mission to deal with my inadequacy and faulty thinking that this relationship would fail like my previous relationships. With that kind of thinking, I was disqualifying myself and overlooking the fact that he wanted to be in a relationship with me. He was the one that said he believed that our relation-ship would please God. Moreover, I knew I had to upgrade my soul, the inner me, to receive what God had presented before me. It was not easy, but it was worth it and necessary. I had to take inventory of what I had to offer him. While I was not as small as other women, my heart was right towards God, and I had a personal relationship with the Father. This meant that God was not just my Savior, but He was Lord over my life.

According to my husband of ten years now, it was my fervent love for Jesus that he found irresistible. He also said that it created a hunger and thirst in him that made him determined to make me his wife. Therefore, as you move forward in the waiting process, don't allow what you have or don't have to discourage you from believing that God will give you, His best. Just as He blessed me, He is waiting to bless you. Go ahead and do the work. Upgrade your inner man from fear to faith and from rejection to acceptance of the Father's love.

I want to challenge each of you to make a commitment to allow the love of God to permeate your heart. To allow His love to flow through you like a river, so it will reach out and touch others. Just like the woman at the well when she met Jesus, and He told her everything about herself. She left her water pot. She left the container that she needed to retrieve water, and she received His love, acceptance, and living water. She went and poured it on others, so they became thirsty and wanted to drink. She became the container that overflowed with God's love (see John chapter 4). They wanted to know, *where is that living water? How can we have that living water that's not subject to a locality?"*

Go forth and be an expression of the Father, so when others see you, you remind them of the Father whose love never runs dry. You are a container full of God's glory. Below are some scriptures to get you started, and you should be able to build from there.

SCRIPTURES:

"Then saith the woman of Samaria unto him, how is it that thou, being a Jew, askest drink of me, which am a woman of Samaria? for the Jews have no dealings with the Samaritans."
"Jesus answered and said unto her, if thou knewest the gift of God, and who it is that saith to thee, Give me to drink; thou wouldest have asked of him, and he would have given thee living water."
"The woman saith unto him, Sir, thou hast nothing to draw with, and the well is deep: from whence then hast thou that living water?"
"Art thou greater than our father Jacob, which gave us the well, and drank thereof himself, and his children, and his cattle?"

"Jesus answered and said unto her, whosoever drinketh of this water shall thirst again:"
"But whosoever drinketh of the water that I shall give him shall never thirst; but the water that I shall give him shall be in him a well of water springing up into everlasting life."
"The woman saith unto him, Sir, give me this water, that I thirst not, neither come hither to draw."
"Jesus saith unto her, Go, call thy husband, and come hither."
"The woman answered and said, I have no husband. Jesus said unto her, Thou hast well said, I have no husband:"
"For thou hast had five husbands; and he whom thou now hast is not thy husband: in that saidst thou truly."
"The woman saith unto him, Sir, I perceive that thou art a prophet."
"Our fathers worshipped in this mountain; and ye say, that in Jerusalem is the place where men ought to worship."
"Jesus saith unto her, Woman, believe me, the hour cometh, when ye shall neither in this mountain, nor yet at Jerusalem, worship the Father."

*"Ye worship ye know not what: we know what
we worship: for salvation is of the Jews."*

*"But the hour cometh, and now is, when the true
worshippers shall worship the Father in spirit and in
truth: for the Father seeketh such to worship Him."*

*"God is a Spirit: and they that worship Him must
worship Him in spirit and in truth."*

*"The woman saith unto Him, I know that Messias
cometh, which is called Christ: when He is come,
He will tell us all things."*

"Jesus saith unto her, I that speak unto thee am He."

*"And upon this came His disciples, and marveled
that He talked with the woman: yet no man said,
What seekest thou? or, why talkest thou with her?"*

*"The woman then left her waterpot, and went her
way into the city, and saith to the men,
Come, see a man, which told me all things
that ever I did: is not this the Christ?"*

–John 4:9-29 KJV

*"There is no fear in love; but perfect love casts out
fear: because fear hath torment. He that feareth is
not made perfect in love."*

–I John 4:18 KJV

*"To the praise of the glory of His grace, wherein
He hath made us accepted in the beloved."*

–Ephesians 1:6 KJV

Prayer

Father, thank you that your love dismantled all fear, and Your acceptance of me has rooted out the spirit of rejection. Thank you that I am accepted by the beloved; therefore, I don't have to walk in fear, doubt, or shame. Your love for me covers every past, present, and future sin. Today, I've decided not to take your love for granted and to allow Your love to flow through me like a river that waters the dry places in my life. In Jesus's name! Amen.

CHAPTER 5

Allow Your Body to Become God's Altar

*"What? Know ye not that your body is the temple
of the Holy Ghost, which is in you, which ye
Have of God, and ye are not your own."*
–1 Corinthians 6:19 KJV

To me, an altar is a safe place, a secret place where you can let your guard down and be true to yourself. It is a place where you can encounter the true and living God; it is a place of authenticity and transparency. It is a place where you can be naked before Him, and you can share your innermost fears knowing that He cares about everything concerning you. The best part is that our secrets are safe with Him. While He may allow others to encourage and speak a word concerning us, only God knows our heart. He knows the real us. In other words, you don't have to hide the longing that is in your soul to connect with someone intimately. You don't have to hide from God when those sexual urges arise. We serve a God who cares about us and permits the desire for sexual intimacy in the confinements of the marital bed. I know it's easier said than done, especially if you have experienced sex outside of what God intended. Even if you had those experiences, you could go before the Throne of Grace and ask a loving Father to wash you with His word and give you the strength to submit your body as a living sacrifice. It says in Romans 12:1 in the Amplified Version of the Bible, "Therefore I urge you, brothers and sisters, by the mercies of God, to present your bodies [dedicating all of yourselves, set apart] as a living sacrifice, holy and well-pleasing to God, which is your rational (logical, intelligent) act of worship." It is an act of worship to God when we choose to wait for sexual relations. Therefore, your body becomes God's altar, a dwelling place for Him to rest, rule, and abide.

MY STORY:

During the first couple years of living for God, I struggled with abstaining from sexual intercourse. One of my struggles was because I already had a child out of wedlock, so I felt like an easy target. When I met men, some automatically assumed that I was still having sex because I had a child. This was so disheartening and discouraging to me that

I asked the Father, "Why should I abstain from sex when I already have a child?" Then, I heard the Holy Spirit say, "Charmia, you are going to be my example on the earth to be a witness that it is possible. It is possible for me to keep you." (Even now, it is possible for God to keep you. He desires for you also to be His example on the earth). Then, He went on to say, "The way you live your life is not just impacting you, but it will also impact your children's children." That's when I made a decision to submit not only my heart but also my body to God for safe keeping. I also decided not to allow different men around my child. My desire was to live an exemplary life before her, so when she became older, she would know that she doesn't have to give her body for love. Then, I began asking God to break every ungodly soul tie trying to prevent me from moving forward in presenting my body to Him. I threw away all gifts, keepsakes, and numbers that connected me to ungodly relationships. I even changed my telephone number. It's funny. I changed my telephone number so many times that my family didn't know how to contact me. Finally, I grew a backbone and took responsibility for my feelings of loneliness and insecurities that led me to these emotional soul ties. In taking responsibility, I stopped changing my telephone numbers. I started apologizing for defrauding these men by having midnight conversations knowing they were not the ones God destined for me (see 1 Corinthians 6:8). I even ceased dating those in whom I knew I would be unequally yoked because I knew we were not God's best for each other.

The answer was never the bed. I had to allow God to send me a mate who was willing to wait until we were married before we embraced the bed. I found that even when I met my future husband, I was trying to prove my love through hugs and kisses only to leave his presence feeling convicted that this was not God's way. He and I both were convicted and agreed to establish boundaries in our courtship. Even though we didn't visit each other in our homes, we met at public parks on several occasions.

ANOTHER STORY:

The Lord revealed to my future husband first that we were compatible with each other. There was also an inner witness in our spirits that we could be suitable for each other. Instantly, we started speaking over the phone and having late night conversations to the point that our conversations were building a fleshly foundation instead of a godly one. How do I know this? We found ourselves leaving home around 11:00pm at night to meet at the park. Each time we met at the park, we would begin to hug and kiss each other until a police officer would interrupt our folly. That happened at every park we visited; the Lord would send a police officer to interrupt our fleshly behavior and force us from the park which was a place of temptation for us. After the third time, the Lord called my husband and I to participate in a 90-day fast to abstain from communicating with each other. God told us that He needed to renew our minds as it related to relationships. He wanted us to return back to Him. The Lord wanted to prepare us separately for what was going to be ahead of us. Therefore, my husband and I had to silence our flesh, so we could hear what the Spirit of God was saying concerning us.

The Lord was desiring to tear down the old paradigms of the worldly way of dating and establish a new standard by which we should abide. Therefore, I was reminded of the scripture in John 12:24 in the Amplified Version of the Bible that says "I assure you and most solemnly say to you, unless a grain of wheat falls into the earth and dies, it remains alone (just one grain, never more). But if it dies, it produces much grain and yields a harvest." My future husband and I chose to let what we thought a relationship should look like die, and we allowed the Holy Spirit to birth something new through us. To be honest, those 90 days of not speaking to my husband over the telephone were challenging, but I did have an opportunity to see him at church. During this time, I kept hearing the Lord say that He wanted to heal my insecurity in thinking that I had to use my body to secure a man. If you have wrestled with insecurities or trust issues in your past, it's important for you to allow the Lord to heal your heart and establish the pace of your relationship.

As a result of my future husband making the decision to fast and deny his flesh for the 18 months of our courtship, God laid the foundation of trust that we are now experiencing in our marriage. Therefore, I'm glad that we were corrected by the Holy Spirit to work the Word instead of our bodies. Society says it's okay to try it before you buy it, but God says that we have been "bought with a price, so we should glorify Him with our bodies" (see 1 Corinthians 6:20). The Word of God also tells us "to be holy because God is holy" (see 1 Peter 1:16). Being holy is not so much about wearing long skirts, abstaining from wearing make-up, or refraining from doing anything that can be observed by the outward appearance. It's an inner reverence of God in our heart which causes our lifestyle to come into alignment with His Word.

Today, I challenge you. If you have not already done so, present your body as a living sacrifice knowing that your body is a sacred place for the Holy Spirit (see Romans 12:1). The Lord will give you clearance on whom to share your altar with. Let me clarify something as it relates to clearance. Your first clearance or approval is spiritual. Before you invite anyone in your life, you should seek clearance from God and your spiritual covering. We should always seek God's approval before we allow anyone in our lives (if I may suggest, pre-marital counseling is essential as well). After receiving God's approval (and confirmation from your spiritual covering), the second approval is the earthly approval by obtaining a license for the bed. Yes, every martial bed requires license. Just like you can't drive a vehicle without a license, why would you allow someone to drive you without a heavenly and earthly commitment? I know I hear someone saying it's okay to test drive the vehicle before you buy it, but if we can be honest, most of us prefer something new versus something that has been used. However, in all fairness, you still need a driver license to test drive a car, so we need license for the bed. When your mate comes, he or she will not only desire your body, but also, he or she will admire your spirit and be compatible with your soul. This day, you have been awakened to the reality that your body is a dwelling place for the Spirit of God.

In counseling with different women and from my personal experience, we discussed how engaging in premarital intercourse can diminish one's self-esteem. I can recall that each time I laid illegally with a man (no martial license), it felt as though I was losing part of my soul. I felt as though I was losing sight of who God had called and created me to manifest in my single season. In doing so, I made man my god, and in Exodus 20:3 it tells us that "we shouldn't have any god before the Lord our God." When we yield to sin, whether it's sexual, emotional, or financial, it becomes a type of god in our lives because it governs us instead of us governing it.

In this hour, you do not have to settle. It's okay to wait on God. It's okay to seek after God. It's okay to wait for love. It's okay to wait for sexual intimacy until you are married. In Hebrews 13:4 it says that "marriage is honorable, and the bed is undefiled." The marriage bed is worth the wait because it's an expression of love and "due benevolence" to your mate (see 1 Corinthians 7:3). Remember, the marital bed is undefiled, which means no one can dictate to you how you should navigate through your bedroom.

When my husband and I got married, I shed blood all over again the night of our honeymoon. I know, right? I'm still trying to figure out how this was scientifically possible. All I know is that God knows how to restore us. He knows how to keep us and make us new again. My earnest prayer was that when my husband and I wed, we would make a covenant by the shedding of blood. Now, that was my desire from the Lord. You may have a different desire, and that's okay. The Lord will give you your own testimony, and we must not compare our testimonies with others but make a decision to glorify God for the way He delivers each of us.

I'll be discussing more about our courtship process in my next book, but for now, I want those of you who are waiting for a spouse to be encouraged.

Wait on love. Continue to allow your body to be God's altar. Below are some scriptures to get you started on your journey.

SCRIPTURES:

"I beseech you therefore, brethren, by the mercies of God, that ye present your bodies a living sacrifice, holy, acceptable unto God, which is your reasonable service."
–Romans 12:1 KJV

"Because it is written, Be ye holy; for I am holy."
–1 Peter 1:16 KJV

"Meats for the belly, and the belly for meats: but God shall destroy both it and them. Now the body is not for fornication, but for the Lord; and the Lord for the body. And God hath both raised up the Lord, and will also raise up us by his own power. Know ye not that your bodies are the members of Christ? shall I then take the members of Christ, and make them the members of an harlot? God forbid. What? know ye not that he which is joined to an harlot is

*one body? for two, saith he, shall be one flesh. But
he that is joined unto the Lord is one spirit. Flee
fornication. Every sin that a man doeth is without
the body; but he that committeth fornication sin-
neth against his own body. What? know ye not that
your body is the temple of the Holy Ghost which is
in you, which ye have of God, and ye are not your
own? For ye are bought with a price: therefore
glorify God in your body, and in your spirit,
which are God's."*

–1 Corinthians 6: 13-20 KJV

Prayer

Father, I present my body as a living sacrifice, holy and acceptable to You, which is my reasonable service. I choose not to be confirmed or fashioned after this world's system. I choose to be transformed by the renewing of my mind, heart, and spirit. Today, I make the decision to allow my body to become Your dwelling place, and I repent if I have not valued what You value. I repent for sharing my body with men (women) who were not my husband (wife), and I chose this day to wait on You. I receive Your love, forgiveness, and grace to be a woman (man) of purity until I am married in Jesus's name. Amen.

CHAPTER 6

Seek Concreteness

*"Call unto me, and I will answer thee,
and I will show the great and mighty things
which thou knowest not."*

– Jeremiah 33:3 KJV

I n chapter one, we discussed that sometimes we get tired of waiting, but we need to ask the Holy Spirit to reveal our hearts and the root of our impatience. In this chapter, we'll talk about calling on the Lord and asking Him to reveal why you are still single. In counseling with single individuals, I often ask this question, *have you ever thought about asking the Lord for the reason behind your singleness?* Several of them answered, *No.* The other responses were, *I pray and thank God daily for sending my mate. I know that God has a plan. I just don't think about it. God knows what I need and when I need it. I know that there is someone out there for me. The most famous response is, there is a short-age of good men.*

Here's my response to these answers:

When you have a revelation of God's love and understand that He desires the best for you, you can go before His Throne of Grace with boldness and asking Him, "Why am I still single?" I remember each time that I asked about my singleness, He would say, "your motives are still not right. Charmia, you want someone in your life to help with the expenses like a business instead of a life partner. You're not ready yet."

I also remember attending one conference after another, searching for the golden answer for my singleness. Finally, one day after basking in the presence of the Father, I asked Him, *why am I still single?* This time, my question was not rooted in fear and rejection or filled with feelings of unworthiness. My heart was open and ready to hear from Heaven because I had a revelation of His love. Then, I went on and asked, *how do I purify my motives and desire a mate not just for financial assistance or just because I'm tired of being the head of my household? How do I transition from this place?* Then, the Lord spoke to my spirit just like He is going to speak to your spirit.

SIDE NOTE:
Hearing the voice of God is so important. One

way you can hear the voice of God is through His Word. When you spend time reading and meditating in the Word, you will receive more of His Spirit. The Bible tells us in John 6:63 that "it is the Spirit that quickeneth, the flesh profiteth nothing: the words that I speak unto you, they are spirit, and they are life." The more you read, the more of Him you will receive. God is a Spirit, and He has made us to be spiritual beings. Therefore, in order to feed the spirit part of us, we must feed it spiritual food which is the Word of God. Also, my prayer is that this book is ministering to the spiritual part of you. I hope it is encouraging you to know that God is no respecter of persons, and what He has done for others and me, He will do for you.

Then, the Lord spoke to me through Psalm 23:1 which says, "The Lord is my Shepherd, and I shall not want." After meditating on this scripture, I received a revelation that I shall not want or lack financial stability. In other words, I didn't have to have a mate to take care of me financially. I didn't have to have a mate just for sexual pleasures. I didn't have to have a mate just to say that my child had a father. Our Heavenly Father desires for us to know that He is a good, good Father. He wants you to know that He will be a Father to your child or children until He sends an earthly Father. The Lord can and will supply all your needs (see Philippians 4:19). "Your Maker is your husband" (see Isaiah 54:5). He is whatever you need Him to be in this season.

MY STORY:

I remember growing through periods of lack, barely enough, and just enough. This was a very frustrating season because I was giving my tithes and seeing little in return. I remember crying out before the Lord and reminding Him of His word. Then, I heard the Lord say, *Trust thou me? I said, Lord, I trust you, but I am tired of having just enough. I remember saying, if you would send me my husband, together, we can have more than enough.*

However, it was through seeking understanding from God that I learned that the Lord desired to prosper me before he positioned me for my mate. Therefore, I began seeking the Lord for another stream of income in addition to my full-time employment. It was through praying, fasting, and standing in the gap for others that the Lord birthed real estate into my spirit. Not only did He speak real estate in my spirit, but He also spoke the name of the brokerage company, and I was thrust into the licensure class the very next day. I was able to close my first deal within 30 days of being licensed. It was then that my motives for finding my mate were purified again, and I no longer desired a financier instead of fiancée. It was also then the Lord proved to me that He was and still is my Provider. He desires to be your Provider as you wait for your mate.

In this hour, the Father is calling us to give Him our hearts and not just our materialistic blessings. He wants us to be honest and transparent before a loving Father who desires to give us the desires of our hearts (see Psalms 37:4). "As we seek the Father, He will be found" (see Isaiah 55:6). "As we knock, the door will be opened to us. As we ask, it shall be given to us" (see Matthew 7:7). The Lord is longing for us to seek and search after Him. Instead of chasing things, the Lord desires for us to thirst after Him, search after Him, and pursue Him like our lives are dependent upon Him, which they are. We are who we are by the grace of God(see 1 Corinthians 15:10).

We must not allow feelings of inadequacy and condemnation to make us feel disqualified, unworthy, or unable to receive from Him. We'll never be worthy of His grace; there's nothing we can do to make ourselves worthy.

What we can do is understand that the presence of God, His Spirit in us, makes us worthy. He makes us valuable. It's the hidden man of the heart that makes us who we are. It's the real us that makes us different and unique before the Father and others.

I remember the Lord telling me that as I pursued Him, He would cause His son (the one who was suitable for me) to pursue after me. While the Lord doesn't choose our mate, He gives us the opportunity to choose based upon the healthiness of our soul. We must allow the Father to not only purify our motives but also to cleanse our heart from the dysfunctions of our past. In other words, the Word of God has the ability to revive, renew, and posture us to hear from Heaven. You are not forgotten. You can hear from God. You can be led by the Spirit of God. Don't allow your past to disqualify your future. Believe today! Decide today to seek concreteness by asking the Lord the reason for your singleness.

As this chapter ends, I challenge you to seek concreteness by asking our Heavenly Father the real questions of your heart. Below are some scriptures to start you on your journey.

SCRIPTURES:

*"The Lord is nigh unto all them that call upon
Him, to all that call upon Him in truth."*
–Psalms 145:18 KJV

*"Seek ye the Lord while He may be found, call
ye upon Him while he is near:"*
–Isaiah 55:6 KJV

*"Call unto Me, and I will answer thee,
and shew thee great and mighty things,
which thou knowest not."*
–Jeremiah 33:3 KJV

*"Then shall ye call upon Me, and ye shall go and
pray unto me, and I will hearken unto you."*
–Jeremiah 29:12 KJV

*"My sheep hear My voice, and I know them,
and they follow Me:"*
–John 10:27 KJV

Prayer

Father, I ask Your forgiveness for pursuing people, places, and things instead of seeking Your kingdom and righteousness, so everything I need will be added unto me. Now, I receive by faith the reason for my singleness. I understand me being single is not because I am unlovable or unworthy. It's because You are perfecting some things in me. And at the appointed time, You will present me before the one who is in agreement with my destiny and compatible with my soul. In Jesus's name. Amen.

CHAPTER 7

Embrace The Wait with Expectancy

"My soul, wait thou only upon God;
my expectation is from him."

–Psalm 62:5 KJV

My definition of waiting is to continue in the assignment to which you were called while waiting with expectancy for the answer to your prayers. To wait on God means to remain faithful to God while waiting on Him to be faithful to His promises, which are already written in His Word. The Word tells us that "God hastens to perform His word" (see Jeremiah 1:12). If we can find a scripture regarding a promise, then we have rights for that promise to be manifested in our lives. As we renew our minds in the area of that promise, our focus will begin shifting from relying on our ability to "casting our cares" upon God (see 1 Peter 5:7). Only God has the ability to bring our desires to pass (see Psalm 37:4). Only God can grant our requests.

Let's stop right here just for one moment. I decree and declare peace over you in the name of Jesus. I release peace over frustration. I release joy over sadness. I release clarity where there is confusion. I release wholeness where there is brokenness. I release love where there is fear and rejection. I release hope for you to believe again, trust again, and desire to love again in Jesus's name.

In order to embrace your waiting season fully, you need to close the curtains again to what others are doing and begin focusing on the Lover of your soul. Focus on the One who gives you all things to enjoy richly. Now, don't misunderstand me. It's okay to admire others; it's okay to celebrate with others. However, if you leave your curtains open too long, you'll begin to feel left out. You'll begin to feel like you've been in this season a little longer than you expected, and others are not doing what you're doing, but they're getting the results you desire. Before you know it, you will have opened the door to envy because you failed to embrace your waiting season. During this time, you must stay away from the comparison trap. You can't compare your life with somebody else's life because the Lord created each of us differently.

- You are different.
- You are God's masterpiece.
- You are chosen.
- You are loved.
- You are being set aside for such a time as this.

As I said earlier, in Jeremiah 29:11, it says that "God knows the thoughts and plans that He has for you." If you ever find yourself at a juncture in your life where you are confused or unsure of which way to go, go back to that scripture. Also, Jeremiah 33:3 says, Call upon Him. It's okay to "call upon the name of the Lord, and He will answer you and show you great and mighty things that you do not know."

Don't allow what's going on with your neighbor to cause you to lose focus. Remain in a place of faith. Remain in a place of expectancy. You must know that waiting on God is not a death, but a life sentence. You're not just waiting, but you're expecting God to fulfill His promises. When you walk out the house, you're in expectation. When you go to the store, you're in expectation. When you go to work, you're in expectation. Right now, some of us are having worship encounters online, but you still should be in expectation because that can't hinder God's plan for your life. There's no failure in God. God cannot fail.

He is unlike any man; therefore, you must not allow your disappointments with mankind to diminish your trust and confidence in God's Word. Although we are made in "His likeness and His image" (see Genesis 1:26), we still make mistakes, but we serve a God who is perfect in all His ways. We can trust Him. For some of us who weren't raised by an earthly Father, we might find it challenging to rely on God because of our past experiences. In those times of struggle, you must take authority of your thoughts and immerse yourself in the truths of God's Word. You must believe that He'll never leave you nor forsake you. You must believe that Heaven and Earth will pass away but not His Word. He is a good, good Father. He will perform it. He will finish what He started in your life. There is nothing too hard for God. He can do anything but fail.

MY STORY:

I remember the Lord leading me on a series of fasting and praying assignments during which I was praying for my mate specifically. I also remember praying a specific scripture found in the book of Isaiah 34:16. Listen, I read that scripture in multiple translations to the point that it became more real to me than anything else. I recited that scripture in the morning, noon, and evening until it was a part of who I was. One day, after my third fast, I heard the Lord say that He was sending my husband to me within the next 90 days. Immediately, I thought that it was my flesh, but in my spirit, I knew that I've never heard the Lord say anything like this before. Therefore, when we receive a word from the Lord, we must begin to seek the Lord for our corresponding action. How do we respond to what the Lord has spoken to us? Faith without action is dead, so when you really receive something in your spirit, it will cause you to respond. Your response will become a prophetic act that demonstrates your faith in what the Lord has said. For example, after I heard the Lord say that He was sending my husband, my response to His word was to call all the men (about 2 of them) who were calling me and tell them that God was sending my husband. I apologized to each one for defrauding and misleading them because of my loneliness. I asked them to forgive me for wasting their time. That was my corresponding action. Get this. The Lord said that

He was sending my husband which meant that the men who were in my life were not destined to be my husband. Why would He send someone who already was here? Hence, I accepted that my husband was on the way and prepared for him by being honest with those other men that they were not the one.

We serve a God who loves and cares about us and who gave His only begotten Son for us that whosoever believes in Him should not perish, but have everlasting life (see John 3:16). Not only that, but He also came that we may have "life in abundance, to the fullest, until it overflows" (see John 10:10 amp). He desires for us to experience overflow in every area of our life.

Now, will it be without scrapes or bruises? No. Will it all be tear-free and carefree? No. However, you must know that better is the ending of a thing than its beginning (see paraphrase Ecclesiastes 7:8). I know some of you were married, and then you found yourself divorced. Some of you didn't have children, and now you have children. Some of you didn't sign up to be a single parent. Some of you didn't sign up to be married for 20 years, and then you had to start all over again.

I'll tell you this. Your situation didn't catch God

by surprise. Jesus is the antidote. He is your healer. He is your soon-coming King. He is the Lover of your soul. You are accepted by Him. His plans for you are better than man's plans. His plans for you are better than your disappointment. His plans for you are better than anything you ever can imagine.

I challenge you today to embrace the wait with expectancy and believe that "no good thing will He withhold from you if you continue to walk righteously before Him" (see Psalms 84:11). Make that your anthem today. The Lord is mindful of you. He loves you, and He has a plan for your life. Below are some scriptures for your mediation.

SCRIPTURES:

"Wait on the Lord be of good courage, and he shall strengthen thine heart: wait, I say, on the Lord."

–Psalms 27: 14 KJV

"Delight thyself also in the Lord; and he shall give thee the desires of thine heart."

–Psalms 37:4 KJV

"For the Lord God is a sun and shield: the Lord will give grace and glory: no good thing will he withhold from them that walk uprightly."

–Psalms 84:11 KJV

"For God so loved the world, that he gave his only begotten Son, that whosoever believeth in him should not perish, but have everlasting life."

–John 3: 16 KJV

Prayer

Father, forgive me for allowing what I see in the natural realm to become more real to me than what You spoke in Your Word. I recommit my heart, mind, and aspirations to You today, and I choose to believe in You and Your Word above everything else. Now, I wait in faith and expectation for Your promise to be fulfilled in my life. In Jesus's name. Amen.

CHAPTER 8

Speak Well over the Waiting Season

"Thou shalt also decree a thing, and it shall be established unto thee: and the light shines upon thy ways."
–Job 22:28 KJV

In this chapter, I want to encourage you to speak life and release positive affirmations over your waiting season. Therefore, you must decree and declare what the Word of God says about you and your promise. In doing so, you must remain in a posture of praise and not allow anyone or anything to transition you from that place. Praise will lead us into worship, and worship will lead us into the presence of God. In the words of my husband, "praise invites the Lord into our presence, and worship takes us into His presence." It's in that place of worship that we tap into the heart, mind, and will of the Father. This is where we are no longer speaking from an earthly mindset because we have opened a new realm of possibilities. Even in your sleep, you find yourself making declarations and decrees that you will not be single always. You are passing through this season just like seasons change from winter, fall, spring, and summer. You are aware that this too shall come to pass.

It is important to seek concreteness from God, so you can identify your current season. Some of you are in a building season in which God is developing some things in your life. Some of you could be in a restoring season in which God is restoring some things that were lost in the vicissitudes of life. Others of you could be in a season in which God is revealing your value, so you won't settle for less than His best. No matter your season, speak life (faith filled words). Don't curse your waiting season. Don't curse your preparation season. Speak well and become like Mary. She said, "Be it done unto me the handmaiden of the Lord" (see Luke 1:38). When the angel came to her and told her that she was going to be with child, immediately, Mary's response was not like Zacharias's response. Mary's response was "behold the handmaid of the Lord; be unto me according to thy word" (see Luke 1:38). His response was, "How could this be? We're old" (see Luke 1:18). He was a priest. He knew the ways and faithfulness of God, so the angel said, "You will be silent" (paraphrase Luke 1:21). There will be times when you won't have anything good to say, and that's when you must remain silent.

When someone is interrogated by law enforcement, and they are read their Miranda Rights. Those rights tell us that we have a right to remain silent because what we say can be held against us. If you can't speak well over your singleness, be silent. If you can't speak well when others are blessed with a mate, just be silent. Be silent until you can "call those things that are not as though they were" (see Roman 4:17). There are certain things we can't release from our mouths because we don't want them to be released in our lives. The Word tells us in Matthew 12:37 "with our words we will be justified, and with our words we can be condemned." Therefore, we must place a guard over our mouth (see Psalm 141:3) and protect our eyes, ears, and mouths which are access points to the entry of our heart.

In this hour, you must speak well over your waiting season. You must speak, *Lord, while I'm waiting on my mate, you are equipping both of us.* You must speak, *Lord. I'm not going to settle or be complacent in my faith. I'm going to pursue You. I'm going to allow You to reveal what you're doing in this hour because my desire is to seek concreteness through-out my singleness.*

Even when you are married, don't stop seeking God. It's okay to ask Him, *what should I be doing in this hour? What is it for me to do? What can I do, God? How can I serve you on another level? Prepare me, God, for when my mate comes, we will add value to one another.* Of course, all that is birthed from a place of prayer because you have positioned yourself to hear God. Therefore, you begin to thank God in advance for your divine encounters. I remember when I heard the Lord say that He was preparing my mate, and He was getting ready to cause my mate to be thrust into my path. It didn't happen the next day, and it didn't happen the following month. About two months later, my future husband was thrust into my path.

You must believe that once you decree a thing, it's going to be established (see Job 22:28). Sometimes, you have to wrestle with your mind and refuse to be shifted from your place of prayer and praise because it's going to catapult you to a place of expectancy. The more you spend intentional time in the presence of God, the easier it becomes to remain in a position of praise and prayer, so you are able to speak well over your season.

If you know you are struggling in your flesh, maybe you need to add some fasting and consecration to your routine. Maybe, there are some things you're watching that may require you to change the channel. Maybe, there are some things on which you are focusing on that are outside the "you" God created you to be therefore, you may need to close curtains. Close the curtains to comparison and become laser focused on what God has placed inside you and what He is doing in this moment. Do whatever you have to do. The Word tells us to "work out our own salvation with fear and trembling" (see Philippians 2:12). You must begin giving the Lord permission and access to the hidden man of the heart. To tell the truth, some of us don't have a faith problem. We have a righteousness problem in which we believe God won't bless us. We don't believe that we can have beauty for our ashes. Let's pause for a minute and begin to make some decrees and declarations and create an atmosphere of faith.

I am the righteousness of God in Christ Jesus (see 2 Corinthians 5:21). I am who God says I am. I am who I am by the grace of God (see 1 Corinthians 15:10). There is nothing I can do in

the flesh to become righteous. I am made right-
eous by the shed blood of Jesus Christ. Because of
Jesus, I am a new creation. Old things have
passed away, and behold all things become new
(see 2 Corinthians 5:17). I may look the same, but
the inner me has been changed. I may live in the
same house, drive the same car, or be employed at
the same job, but I am different. I am God's child.
His love for me doesn't have limits. His love for
me is unconditional, but His blessings are condi-
tional. Therefore, I live for God not by force, but
by choice.

As you believe, receive, and decree His Word, your spirit will come in alignment with His Word. He desires not only to be God to you, but also to be the Lord of your life. As you allow Him to dwell in your heart, your motives for why you do what you do will begin to change. In other words, you are not serving the Lord, so you can be blessed. You are serving Him because you are blessed already. You are not living a celibate lifestyle, so God can bless you with a mate. You are living a celibate lifestyle, because you understand that your body is the temple of the Lord, and you value what He values. Even now, as I am typing, I hear the Lord saying that some of you have lost your confidence in Him because you have misplaced your confidence in earthly things instead of the Word of God.

MY STORY:

I used to feel confident when I had long extensions, but I was less confident when I wore my natural hair. I used to feel confident when others told me that I did well, but I felt less confident when I didn't receive compliments. I used to feel confident when I was giving my body to men, but I was less confident when I felt the Lord leading me to be celibate. I used to feel confident when I had money in the bank, but I was less confident when I was living paycheck to paycheck. It was then when the Lord asked me if I was living for the praises of men or for the glory of God? Sometimes, we must ask ourselves, "am I living for the amens or the well done my good and faithful servant?" I had to decide to place my confidence in things that are eternal instead of the temporary things in this natural realm, which are subject to change. Therefore, we must hold on to the Word of God as if our life depends on it. The Word tells us that "man does not live or exist by bread alone (natural resources) but by every word that is spoken by God" (see

Matthew 4:4). When you truly accept and receive the Word of God, it's impossible for your life to remain the same. It is impossible for your language to remain the same. It becomes impossible for you to curse your waiting season because of your newly found confidence in the Word of God. Your confidence comes as a result of you meditating and pondering upon the Word of God. This is where the *logos* of God's Word become *rhema*. Rhema simply means the Word of God has been made alive in you and where your spirit man has been awakened. You will find yourself more conscientious of the spiritual realm instead of the natural realm or current circumstance.

I would like to leave you with some scriptures, and 1 John 5:14-15 is one of my favorite scriptures.

SCRIPTURES:

"And this is the confidence that we have in him, that, if we ask anything according to his will, he heareth us: And if we know that he hear us, whatsoever we ask, we know that we have the petitions that we desired of him."

–1 John 5:14-15 KJV

"Death and life are in the power of the tongue: and they that love it shall eat the fruit thereof."
–Proverbs 18:21 KJV

"For by thy words thou shalt be justified, and by thy words thou shalt be condemned."
–Matthew 12:37 KJV

"And when he came out, he could not speak unto them: and they perceived that he had seen a vision in the temple: for he beckoned unto them and remained speechless."
–Luke 1:22 KJV

"Thou shalt also decree a thing, and it shall be established unto thee: and the light shall shine upon thy ways."
–Job 22:28 KJV

Prayer

Father, I cancel every negative word that has proceeded from my mouth, and I ask forgiveness for speaking my opinion instead of the Word of God. Today, I choose to speak life over my waiting seasons. I choose to receive Your predestined plan for my life. I decree and declare that I am enough. I am chosen. I am not forgotten. I will wait patiently upon You, Lord in the name of Jesus. Amen.

CHAPTER 9

Discover the Joy in Waiting

*"Thou will show me the path of life: in thy
presence is fullness of joy; at thy right hand there
are pleasures for evermore."*

–Psalm 16:11 KJV

How's your joy during this season? Is your glass barely empty or half full? If your answer is that it is barely empty, in this chapter, we'll discuss ways to increase your joy, so your glass, which is your spirit, will begin overflowing in the fruit of the Spirit. If you are still single, this is a great time to allow the Lord to prune certain areas of your life, so your life may yield more fruit. Therefore, you must not become offended by the pruning of the Lord. It's okay to yield to the Lord. Allow Him to remove people, places, and things that are not producing fruit and have become stale in your life. The pruning is necessary to position you for your next blessing. In Galatians 5:22-23, the Bible tells us, "The fruit of the Spirit is love, joy, peace, long suffering, gentleness, goodness, faith, meekness, temperance: against such there is no law."

For the sake of this chapter, we will focus on the fruit of joy. While focusing on the fruit of joy, we must understand the process of how one bears fruit. As I think about bearing fruit, I think about a garden or the ground. In order to produce fruit, the fruit must be planted in good soil or plowable ground. For example, the Word of God is seed, and we are to plant the Word in our heart, which is the ground. However, our hearts cannot be contaminated with unbelief, unforgiveness, regret, resentment, hatred, insecurity, jealousy, and envy just to name a few. How can a heart produce fruit if the above items have hardened our ground? Therefore, we must allow the Word of God to till our heart, but we first must recognize that God is not the one to blame. Oftentimes, it was our decisions or poor choices of others that either indirectly or directly affected us or our situations. Then, we must acknowledge that no matter what we have experienced in life, there is still nothing too hard for God. God can cause all things that we have experienced or will experience to work together for our good (see Romans 8:28). While it may not feel good, the Lord knows how to work all things out for our good. In other words,

God can take our mess and make a miracle from it. God can take our sadness and give us gladness. God knows how to give us double for our trouble.

One way to discover your joy in waiting is deciding to forgive. Forgive yourself. Forgive God. Forgive those who have wronged you. If you don't know how to forgive or need help with the forgiving process, it's okay to reach out to God first and then allow the Holy Spirit to lead you to a counselor, mentor, pastor, or friend to walk with you through this process. Forgiveness is for us, so we can live. I remember the Lord telling me that if I don't forgive others for their wrongdoing, I could relive those experiences unconsciously. In other words, I would open myself up to repeating the same behaviors and preventing future growth and development while the offender is living life like it's golden (just a figure of speech). I wasn't hurting him or her, but I was suppressing my newly found joy in Jesus Christ.

In these times, we must remember all that the Lord has done for us. We must remember that He sent His only begotten Son to die for us. In the midst of our disobedience and when they were saying, "Crucify Him," Jesus said to the Father, "Forgive them for they know not what they do."

(see Luke 23:34) Today, the Lord is tugging on your heart to forgive those who have wronged you. He is not asking you to overlook their behaviors because you definitely need to discuss what happened and establish appropriate boundaries as needed. However, He is asking you to forgive them and return back to that place of joy and resting in His love for you.

After asking and receiving God's forgiveness, another way to discover your joy is by spending time with the Lord. It's not necessarily quantitative but qualitative time. Five minutes of undisturbed and undistracted time is better than 20 minutes of meditating on the cares of this world. In other words, spending quality time with the Lord is not so much about what you say to Him. It is more important to hear what He says to you. Spending time with God in prayer shouldn't be a monologue but a dialogue. You say something to Him, and then you wait for Him to say something back to you. What happens if you don't hear anything the first time? Don't give up. Have a conversation with Him in faith and believe in faith that He will respond.

If we can be honest, sometimes, fear will cause us to talk excessively without providing an opportunity for God to respond. Why? Sometimes, we are afraid of God's response, or we have a perception of His response (sometimes faulty), and we are not ready to receive the truth. How do you transition from that place? I would say you can transition from that place by meditating on God's love for you. I know that I mentioned the love of God in an earlier chapter, but I am persuaded that we serve a multi-dimensional God. Every new level or advancement in God requires Him to reveal another dimension of Himself. We will never exhaust knowing all of God because He has no ending or beginning. Therefore, we are always in a place of learning, relying, seeking, and waiting for God's will to be perfected in our life.

Think about this. If while in the presence of God, you find yourself telling Him about what happened six months ago, that could very well mean that you haven't been communicating with Him. For example, when you communicate with someone often, like once a day or every other day, you don't have to catch up. I'm not saying that we should become like a robot in a relationship with God, but I am saying when it comes to our relationship with Him, we should communicate daily with a spirit of honesty and authenticity. He already knows our ending from the beginning, but He desires for us to take pleasure in having a fruitful relationship with Him.

Another way to discover your joy is to practice His presence. In practicing His presence, you become more God-aware than self-aware. In other words, you become mindful that God is always present. Here's the challenge. Begin practicing His presence at least three times a day. For those of you who already are acknowledging His presence, I challenge you to go deeper. Then, allow it to become organic and not forced. Someone may say, *I don't have time for this.* How about trying this while using the restroom or commuting to work? After you have found your rhythm, I encourage you to establish consistency. I believe that our consistency with God will cause both breakthroughs and blessings to invade our lives. If we are consistent in seeking God, He will be consistent in seeking after us. The Word tell us that if we "draw nigh to God, He will draw nigh unto us" (see James 4:8). If you desire to build trust in any relationship, it is built through consistent behaviors.

MY STORY:

At one time, I used to think, if someone was not calling me or asking me for something, how could I have joy? If

I'm not accomplishing this or celebrating this, how could I have real joy? If my children are not on the honor roll, if this wasn't going right, or if my bills were due, how could I have joy? Then, it was hard for me to be sincerely joyous for others because I felt that being joyous for others was subtracting from what the Lord could do for me. Worst of all, I became a manipulator. When others were blessed, I had a sad story, so I could make them feel guilty about their blessing. I also created relationships in which others didn't feel comfortable sharing their testimonies with me. It was my manipulative spirit that caused me to devalue the blessings that God was sending in my life, and my heart of self-pity was reinforcing my manipulation, which was canceling out my joy in Christ. Therefore, I cried before the Lord. He heard me and delivered me from self-pity and manipulation. While I can recognize that spirit, (you will also) I encourage others who I counsel to be grateful for what they have and continue to walk in a spirit of humility. Pride will us behaving like we're entitled to something, but grace helps us understand that God doesn't owe us anything. We owe Him everything. For it is of the Lord's goodness that we are not consumed by our enemies (see Lamentations 3:22-23) or the "inner me", which can be our greatest enemy. I like to say it this way it's always been me against me because I have been my worst critic, yet I can be my greatest supporter.

The Bible tells us in Psalms 16:11, that in the Lord's presence, we can experience an overflowing of joy. There's another scripture that talks about the joy of the Lord being strength to us (see Nehemiah 8:10). Therefore, as you ask God for forgiveness, forgive others and begin practicing the presence of the Lord. You will begin to experience His unspeakable joy. He will become your Source. He will become your stabilizer and your equalizer. I heard some time ago that happiness is based on what is happening, and joy is about what has happened already. Joy comes from knowing that God gave Jesus all power, and when He rose, He gave us the same power. We are never powerless or defeated with Jesus living inside us. We cannot have joy without Jesus.

Have you received Jesus as your Lord and Savior? If you haven't, please take a moment and pray this prayer with me. Lord, Jesus I ask for forgiveness of my sins, and You said in Romans 10:9-10, "If thou shalt confess with thy mouth the Lord Jesus, and shalt believe in thine heart that God hath raised Him from the dead, thou shalt be saved. For with the heart man believeth unto right-eousness; and with the mouth confession is made unto salvation." If you prayed this prayer, then you are saved. Your next step is to connect with a church in your area that will begin to teach and train you in the Word of God. For now, I celebrate your decision and pray that you will continue to grow in the Lord.

Joy is a decision. You must decide to be joyful. You must decide to be positive. It's a choice. You must decide this day to rejoice no matter what life brings your way. You can have joy in your waiting season. You can have peace in your waiting season. You don't have to settle because you feel uncomfortable. You don't have to settle because it's taking a while. You can have comfort. You can have joy. I release joy right now over each of you in the mighty name of Jesus.

Below are some scriptures for your mediation that will continue to build your faith.

SCRIPTURES:

"Thou wilt shew me the path of life: in thy presence is fullness of joy; at thy right hand there are pleasures for evermore."

–Psalm 16:11 KJV

"Then said Jesus, Father, forgive them; for they know not what they do. And they parted his raiment and cast lots."

–Luke 23: 34 KJV

"But the fruit of the Spirit is love, joy, peace, longsuffering, gentleness, goodness, faith, Meekness, temperance: against such there is no law.
And they that are Christ's have crucified the flesh with the affections and lusts.
If we live in the Spirit, let us also walk in the Spirit.
Let us not be desirous of vain glory, provoking one another, envying one another."

–Galatians 5:22-26 KJV

"Draw nigh to God, and he will draw nigh to you. Cleanse your hands, ye sinners; and purify your hearts, ye double minded."

–James 4:8 KJV

Prayer

Lord Jesus, I ask Your forgiveness for trying to live life on my terms. I ask that You create in me a clean heart and renew a right spirit within me. I receive Your forgiveness and recommit my mind, will, and soul to You. I ask that You lead, guide, and restore unto me the joy of my salvation in Jesus's name. Amen

CHAPTER 10

Don't Settle: You Are Worth The Wait

"Seek ye out the book of the Lord, and read: no one of these shall fail, none shall want her mate: for my mouth it hath commanded, and his spirit it hath gathered them."

– Isaiah 34:16 KJV

I n this last chapter, I would like to strengthen your faith and leave you with these words. "Don't settle, you are worth the wait."

Say it with me. I will not settle because I am worth the wait. Say it again. "I will not settle because I am worth the wait.

Why are you worth the wait? You are worth the wait because you understand that you are God's son or daughter. You understand that you are a royal priesthood and a chosen nation created for good works and to bring glory to God(see 1 Peter 2:9). If you've been waiting for any length of time, be encouraged that the longer the wait, the greater the blessing. I waited for 13 1/2 years before my husband and I crossed paths, and if I was required to do it all over again, it would be my pleasure. While my testimony is that he was worth the wait, I hope he still believes that I was worth the wait.

MY STORY:

Prior to getting married, I used to change churches like I was changing clothes. I had to learn that I couldn't manipulate the process, and I couldn't rush the timing of the Lord. Honestly, I learned the hard lessons while trying to birth an Ishmael instead of waiting for my Isaac. While trying to rush my waiting process, I ran into one disappointment after another disappointment. My flesh was trying to take hold of me in this area. However, what was the truth? The truth was I didn't trust God. The truth was that my biological clock was ticking. The truth was I got tired of people telling me to wait on God. I got tired of hearing myself say, "I'm waiting on God." Out of my frustration, I got serious with the Lord. I began to seek understanding about why I was single so long. *Was there something wrong with me? Was I not beautiful enough? Was I too big? Was I too spiritual? Should I dummy myself down and act like I didn't know the Word of God so I can attract a godly man? Should I show more cleavage? Should I act like I was sexually active even though I was not? Lord, I'm tired of changing churches. I desire wholeness in the inner part of me. Lord, just tell me that I am enough. Just let me know that you desire for me to have a husband. Lord, speak to me.*

I heard the Lord say, "Believe thou me? I said," Yes Lord." He asked me again, "Believe thou me?" I said, "Lord, you are right." I prayed several times, but I never prayed in faith believing that I received what I requested from God. I was always trying to make it happen in the flesh when my assignment from God was first to birth it in the Spirit, and from the Spirit, it would manifest in the natural. Therefore, I repented of my dead works and asked God to create in me a clean heart, and He renewed a right Spirit within me (see Psalm 51:10). He renewed a Spirit of faith in me. Shortly thereafter, the Holy Spirit led me to several scriptures regarding marriage that focused on the Lord keeping His promises. With these scriptures, I began to build a prayer strategy and decided to decree and declare these scriptures every day. I created a three-page research paper that expressed the heart of God towards me concerning a mate. Each time I read that declaration; I felt the inner me being strengthened. In other words, my faith level was rising, and faith filled words began to flow unconsciously from my mouth. Why? Out of the abundance of your heart your mouth will speak (see Matthew 12:34). I know some people like to talk, but how they respond will reveal what's in their heart.

Therefore, my response to not having any men calling me was, *any day now.* My response to the lonely nights was *any day now.* My response to being a single parent with no child support was, *any day now.* My response to going to the movies and dining alone at the restaurant was, *any day now.* Before I knew it, I was reciting Isaiah 34:16 three times a day: once in the morning, noon, and evening. I had an *any day now* conviction in my spirit. As you are reading this chapter, you should have an *any day now* conviction in your spirit.

Listen, Isaiah 34:16 came to pass. I didn't have to make it happen. My husband was thrust into my path. I was sitting down at church one Sunday at this particular ministry, and the pastor said, "Charmia, come and be Eve, and Tory [my now-husband], you be Adam." Immediately, my spirit leaped, and I knew that he was the one. I can't explain it scientifically, but I can tell you that when you spend time not only in the presence of God but also in the Word of God, you will develop a sensitivity to the leading of the Lord. As a result of months of fasting and praying, my faith was that the Holy Spirit would bear witness (an inner peace) when my future husband and I crossed paths. While my next book will include what the courtship process looked like for us, I will leave you with this. After my spirit bore witness that we could be compatible, it was up to him and me to have lengthy conversations. It's not enough to have just a spiritual connection, but what does this look like in the natural realm? We had to ask the hard questions. Are we just spiritually compatible but have nothing else in common? Our desire was for compatibility in both areas; therefore, our courtship process was an integral part of us finalizing our future together.

While you're waiting on God, you're not just twiddling your thumbs. You're waiting on God because you're learning how to be true to yourself. While you're waiting on God and not settling, you're learning to close the door to deception. Your mate will come, and he or she will be thrust into your path. During this time, don't settle. Focus on the inner you, which is the real you. That focus will help you attract and recognize who is a good fit for you. Also, take inventory of your strengths and weaknesses. Then, know yourself. Discover your likes and dislikes. Discover your favorite color. Discover your favorite restaurant. It's okay to assess and analyze your behaviors to ensure that they are aligned with your purpose and call of God upon your life.

When I learned how to focus all my attention on our Heavenly Father and allow Him to change those things in me, I began to understand the purpose of my wait. Each year of my wait was designed to prepare me for what was coming next in my life. Don't despise the waiting. Even now, your wait is preparing you. God is preparing you for His best. It's like entering the doctor's office. When you first enter the office, you walk into a waiting area. There, you have patients with and without a spouse who are waiting to see the doctor. There are patients with and without children who are waiting to be seen. Everyone is waiting, so it's easy to start counting how many people are before you, who's after you, and how many people just walked in the office? Before you know it, you have become anxious. Now, you are saying to yourself, am *I next? When am I going to be next? How long is the wait?*

All the above questions are racing through your

mind while you are in the waiting area, but when the nurse calls your name, something shifts. You become excited because it's finally your turn to visit with the physician. Even right now, God is calling your name and bringing you into His eternal private room where He is waiting for you. He is waiting to commune with you. He is waiting for you to draw near to Him. He is waiting for you to call on Him. He is bringing you into His private setting where it's just you and Him. It's like being in a supernatural room where you are not only in communion with the Heavenly Father, but also, He's speaking to the core of your being. You can feel His presence all around you. He's telling you that you are loved. He's telling you that you are accepted by your Beloved. He's telling you not to settle. He's telling you that there is a due season for you.

Let's pause. *I would like for you to allow the Lord to wrap Himself around you. Take a moment to allow the Lord to minister to you and write down what you hear and feel the Holy Spirit saying to you. Don't rush. Take advantage of this time to be with the Holy Spirit. Take advantage of this time to be real before a God who never judges or condemns you. Receive His unconditional love for you.*

By now, you should be in a place where you're ready for the Great Physician and the best Matchmaker because He knows how to do it, and He will bring you through it. Don't despise your waiting season. **Don't settle because you are worth the wait.** You are a jewel. You are the apple of God's eye. He has not forgotten about you.

SCRIPTURES:

"Seek ye out of the book of the Lord, and read: no one of these shall fail, none shall want her mate: for my mouth it hath commanded, and His spirit it hath gathered them."
–Isaiah 34:16 KJV

"Create in me a clean heart, O God; and renew a right spirit within me. Cast me not away from thy presence; and take not thy holy spirit from me. Restore unto me the joy of thy salvation; and uphold me with thy free spirit."
–Psalms 51:10-12 KJV

"A good man out of the good treasure of the heart bringeth forth good things: and an evil man out of the evil treasure bringeth forth evil things.
But I say unto you, That every idle word that men shall speak, they shall give account thereof in the day of judgment. For by thy words thou shalt be justified, and by thy words thou shalt be condemned."

–Matthew 12:34-37 KJV

"But ye are a chosen generation, a royal priesthood, an holy nation, a peculiar people; that ye should shew forth the praises of Him who hath called you out of darkness into His marvelous light;"

–1 Peter 2:9 KJV

Prayer

Father, forgive me for thinking about settling for anything less than Your best. I ask You now to flood my heart with Your love, joy, acceptance, and peace while I rest in this new place of expectancy. Help me to rely on the Holy Spirit to cause my mate and I paths to cross at the appointed time. This day, I choose to wait in faith with joy and expectation that at any day, time, or hour, I will meet my mate in Jesus's name.

Word of Encouragement

Be the light that draws others to Jesus. Be the salt that preserves your home, your children, your community, and your place of employment. Shine while you are waiting because you are worth the wait. Don't settle. God has a mate for you.

THE CONCLUSION

My prayer is that this book has stirred up your spirit, and now, you feel empowered for the wait. I pray that where you were discouraged, you have become encouraged. I pray that where you were weak, you have been strengthened. I pray that where you were hopeless, your hope has been renewed. I pray that where you were ashamed, you are now bold in your confession and ability to stand for God through it all.

Now, I decree and declare Ephesians 1:17-19 over you when it says, "The God of our Lord Jesus Christ, the Father of glory, may give unto you the spirit of wisdom and revelation in the knowledge of him. The eyes of your understanding being enlightened; that ye may know what is the hope of his calling, and what the riches of the glory of his inheritance in the saints, and what is the exceeding greatness of his power to us-ward who believe, according to the working of his mighty power."

May the Lord our God enlighten and open the eyes of your heart to be persuaded fully that you are not forgotten. Although it's been a while, you must believe that you are worth the wait. Your mate is worth the wait. Therefore, embrace this waiting season in faith and expectation with a posture of praise knowing that any day or moment, it will be your turn.

ACKNOWLEDGMENTS

First, I would like to give honor to my Lord & Savior Jesus Christ who graced me with the strength and ability to write this book.

Thank you to my best friend, husband, and Apostle, Tory Q. Martin. None of this would have been possible without your love and support. I am grateful to God for blessing us with six wonderful children and a beautiful grandchild.

To my Kingdom of God Empowerment Center family, thank you so much for your support and standing in the gap through the birthing of this book.

A special thank you to my spiritual mother, Lady Angela Burney, and to my mentors Lady Charlotte Rummage and Ms. Rhonda Miller. I want to give another special thank you to my family, friends, prayer partners, and Charmia Martin Ministry partners.

Another special thank you to Jasmine Womack, CEO of the Empact Group, for guiding me through the writing process. Also, thank you to Dr. Joel Boyce & Lady Latrilla Nolan for the countless hours you spent editing my book.

ABOUT THE AUTHOR

Charmia Martin is a pastor, entrepreneur, social worker, and Christian life coach based in Columbus, Georgia. She is the co-founder of 5 Star Barbershop, LLC and owner of Charmia Martin Realty as well as the Kingdom Life Coaching and Mentoring Program, which focuses on the spiritual and relational development of the individual through empowering, inspiring, and propelling individuals forward in their God-given assignments.

Charmia is a Georgia native who has more than 25 years of ministry experience and serves alongside her husband, Apostle Tory Martin, at the Kingdom of God Empowerment Center. It's through this ministry that they equip and train believers to discern the voice of God and follow His teachings. Together, the couple has six children and one grandchild, all of whom keep them on the move.

Charmia holds both a Bachelor of Arts degree and a Master of Arts degree in Social Work with a professional licensure. Through her years of service, she has helped countless women transition from hoping for change to becoming the epitome of change. Charmia is now a sought-after Christian Life Coach who is known for guiding singles through the turbulence of a broken relationship to emotional wholeness by understanding themselves and empowering them to be their best, authentic selves at all times.

Made in the USA
Columbia, SC
13 May 2024

35238938R00065